AF572538

MARVEL'S
MARVEL
COMICS
FINEST

SALVADOR LARROCA AND ART THIBERT
COVER ART

BOBBIE CHASE
ORIGINAL SERIES EDITOR

POLLY WATSON
REPRINT EDITOR

BOB HARRAS
EDITOR IN CHIEF

COMICRAFT'S JOHN MARASIGAN
DESIGN

RETURN OF THE HEROES™ Contains material originally published in magazine form as HEROES REBORN: THE RETURN #1-4. Published by MARVEL COMICS; 387 PARK AVENUE SOUTH, NEW YORK, N.Y. 10016. Printed in the U.S.A. First Printing, January, 1999. ISBN #0-7851-0705-3. GST #R127032852.

10 9 8 7 6 5 4 3 2 1

RETURN OF THE HEROES

INTRODUCTION

OF TRAGEDIES AND MIRACLES

The scene was grisly, the outcome grim. A world full of bright costumes and brighter hope — was no more.

What does it take to destroy Marvel's first family, the Fantastic Four? What kind of power is needed to vanquish the earth's mightiest heroes, the Avengers? Who could prompt the mutant outlaw X-Men to seek the aid of every hero in New York?

The shocking answer to all of these questions is the same: Onslaught, a being composed of the combined energies of the mutant Magneto's evil psyche and the repressed anger of telepath Professor Charles Xavier, leader of the X-Men and a man respected for his peaceful ideology.

The might and strength of the assembled heroes, including the Fantastic Four and the Avengers, reached only one realization — the sole way to stop Onslaught from furthering his own power, and causing more damage to the entire city of New York, would be through the ultimate sacrifice. Thus the non-mutant heroes hurled themselves into Onslaught with the hope that they would be able to disrupt the fabric of his very being. The heroic gambit paid off, but not without a terrible cost — all those who had jumped into Onslaught had seemingly perished as the rest of the world looked on!

A year later, after much mourning and suffering, all was revealed to be not quite as it seemed. Instead of dying within Onslaught, the heroes had actually been whisked away into another reality created by Franklin Richards, the mutant son of Reed and Sue Richards of the Fantastic Four. In this alternate world the heroes lived new lives which were, to the best of their knowledge, a continuation of their normal lives. They were completely unaware of their previous existence back in the real Marvel Universe.

What you are about to read is how all that changed, the story behind the miracle: how one small boy with the power of a god had the ability to do what no one else could — return the heroes.

The Judgment

Chapter One

THE BEGINNING OF A TYPICALLY ATYPICAL DAY AT THE BAXTER BUILDING, HEADQUARTERS OF THE FANTASTIC FOUR IN NEW YORK CITY...
I HATE YOU, REED RICHARDS.
Hmmm?
YOU HAVE NO BUSINESS LOOKING THAT "TOGETHER" FIRST THING IN THE MORNING.
SUSAN! ARE YOU ALL RIGHT?
SURE. *YAWN* LOUSY DREAMS, THAT'S ALL. AND MY MOUTH TASTES LIKE TOXIC WASTE.
MAYBE I SHOULD GO BACK TO BED...
IF THAT'S WHAT YOU PREFER, BY ALL MEANS.
BUT YOU'RE GOING TO MISS A BEAUTIFUL DAY!
MORNING PEOPLE. SHEESH.
NOT A CLOUD IN THE SKY. THE KIND OF WEATHER THAT MAKES YOU GLAD TO BE ALIVE.

STAN LEE PRESENTS:
HEROES REBORN
THE RETURN PART 1 OF 4
IN ANOTHER NEW YORK, NEAR A FORMER HEADQUARTERS OF OUR JUST MENTIONED HEROES...
THE JUDGMENT
PETER DAVID WRITER
SALVADOR LARROCA PENCILER
ART THIBERT INKER
RICHARD STARKINGS & COMICRAFT/KF LETTERS
STEVE BUCCELLATO COLORS
POLLY WATSON ASS'T EDITOR
BOBBIE CHASE EDITOR
BOB HARRAS CHIEF

I WANT MY MOMMY AND DADDY!

YOU DO NOT NEED REED AND SUSAN RICHARDS.
YES! YES, I **DO!** I WANT THEM AND I WANNA **BE** WITH THEM!
UNNECESSARY. YOU WILL BE WITH US.

BUT WE KNOW IT IS YET DIFFICULT FOR YOU TO COMPREHEND. SO WE ARE MAKING CONTACT WITH YOU IN A WAY YOU WILL UNDERSTAND.

BUT I ***DON'T*** UNNERSTAND! I DON'T UNNERSTAND ***ANY*** OF THIS!
DO NOT WORRY. YOU WILL.

NO! GET ***AWAY*** FROM ME! I'M NOT S'POSED TO TALK TO ***STRANGERS!***
GET AWAY RIGHT N--

WHOAAAAA!

YOU HAVE POWERS YOU DO NOT FULLY UNDERSTAND YET, FRANKLIN RICHARDS. POWERS TO SHAPE REALITY.
POWERS UNPRECEDENTED IN YOUR RACE'S HISTORY.
BUT WITH THAT POWER COME HARD CHOICES.
IT IS TIME FOR YOU TO REALIZE THAT YOUR PARENTS ARE ELSEWHERE AND ELSEWHEN... BUT YOU CAN REACH THEM.
YOU PUT THEM THERE. YOU SHUNTED THEM INTO ANOTHER WORLD.
AND YOU CAN BRING THEM BACK TO A WORLD, IF YOU SO DESIRE. BUT YOU WILL HAVE TO DECIDE WHAT SORT OF WORLD IT WILL BE.
IT WILL BE A DECISION... OF COSMIC PROPORTIONS.

"FOR NOW, HOWEVER... RETURN TO YOUR PRESENT ABODE. RETURN TO THE SWAMP IN FLORIDA...
"...WHERE YOUR CURRENT GUARDIAN -- THE MAN-THING -- TENDS TO YOU.
"BUT DO NOT FORGET THIS DREAM.

"SLEEP, FRANKLIN... CLUTCHING THE BLUE BALL, THE MEANING OF WHICH YOU SENSE ON ONLY A RUDIMENTARY LEVEL.
"AND I SHALL BE ALONG PRESENTLY...
"...SO THAT YOU WILL SEE THE LIGHT."
NO... G'WAY...
DON'T WANNA... GO WITH YOU...

...SEE ANY... STUPID LIGHT...

LIGHT?

IT'S... MORNING...
WHERE'S MY..?

NO!

FRANKLIN SEES THE BALL VANISH BENEATH THE WATER, INTO THE GULLET OF THE SWAMP DENIZEN.
AND HE IS IMMEDIATELY SEIZED WITH A PRIMAL TERROR:
NOT UNDERSTANDING HIS CONNECTION TO, NOR THE IMPORTANCE OF THE BALL...
...BUT NONETHELESS FEARFUL OF LOSING IT.
AND THE PRESENCE OF FEAR IS MORE THAN ENOUGH TO DRAW OUT THE MAN-THING...
...THE MUCK MONSTER, GUARDIAN OF THE NEXUS OF ALL REALITIES, WHOSE PATH HAS CROSSED THAT OF FRANKLIN RICHARDS, AND WHO HAS BROUGHT HIM HERE TO THE SWAMP FOR PROTECTION.
BUT THE MAN-THING'S MEMORY IS TRANSITORY AT BEST, AND EASILY DISMISSED WHEN OTHER CONSIDERATIONS ARE BROUGHT FORWARD. MOST PARTICULARLY, CONSIDERATIONS SUCH AS...
...FEAR. FEAR, WHICH THE MAN-THING REVILES. FOR WHATEVER KNOWS FEAR... BURNS AT THE MAN-THING'S TOUCH. FEAR...
...WHICH POURS FORTH FROM FRANKLIN LIKE BILE... AND WHICH TURNS HIS PROTECTOR...
...INTO A THREAT.

QUEENS, NEW YORK...

HEY, AUNT ANNA... MIND PUTTING ON THE *WEATHER CHANNEL?*

SEE IF THERE'S ANY HINT AS TO WHEN THIS *DOWNPOUR'S* GOING TO LET UP?

I'D JUST LIKE TO FINISH WATCHING THIS REPORT ON CNN, PETER...

Oh, SURE. WHAT'S IT ABOUT?

WELL, IT'S ABOUT ALL THOSE POOR *HEROES.* IT'S THE ANNIVERSARY OF THEIR...

...THEIR *DEATHS,* YOU KNOW.

YEAH. I KNOW.

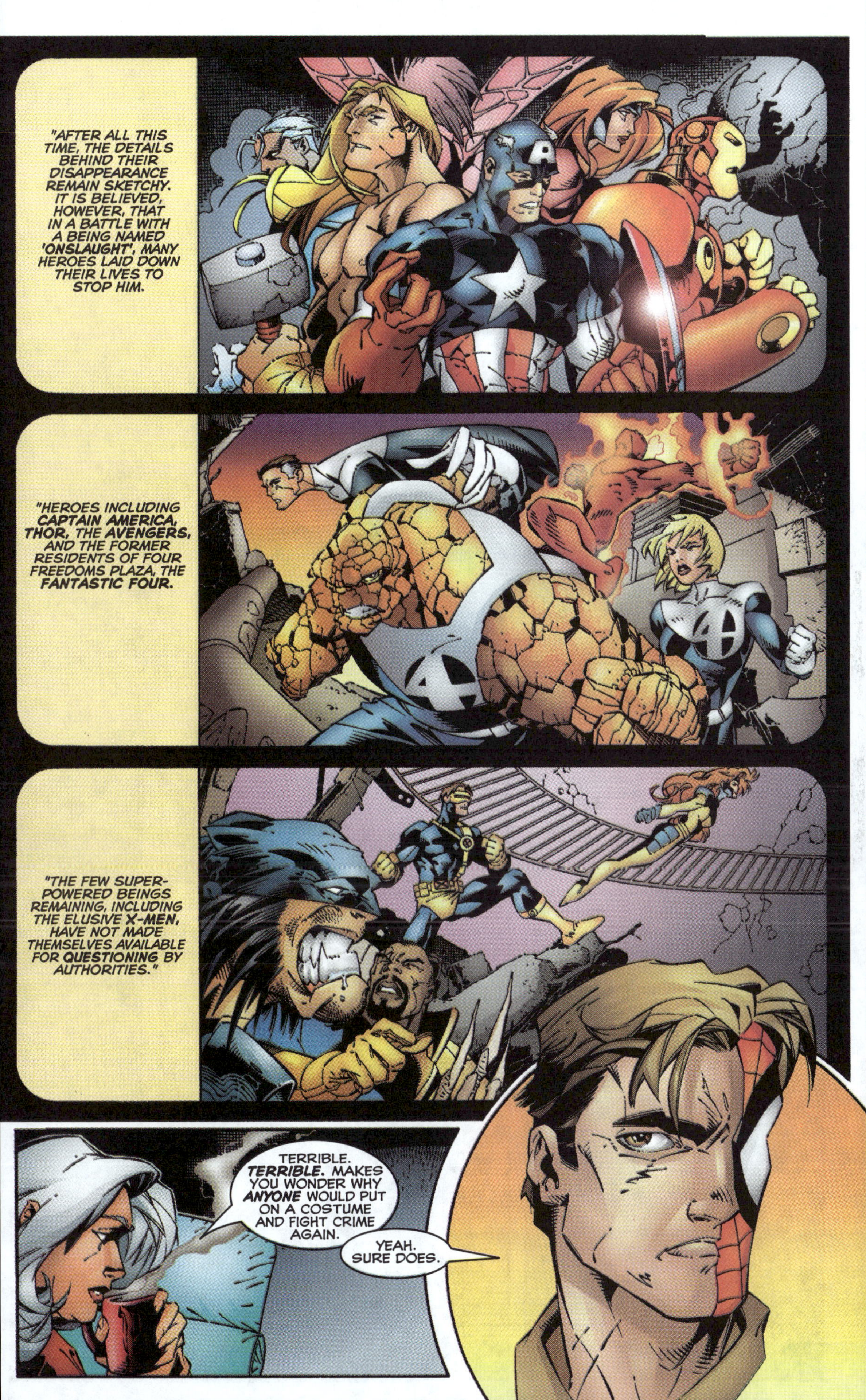
"AFTER ALL THIS TIME, THE DETAILS BEHIND THEIR DISAPPEARANCE REMAIN SKETCHY. IT IS BELIEVED, HOWEVER, THAT IN A BATTLE WITH A BEING NAMED 'ONSLAUGHT', MANY HEROES LAID DOWN THEIR LIVES TO STOP HIM.
"HEROES INCLUDING CAPTAIN AMERICA, THOR, THE AVENGERS, AND THE FORMER RESIDENTS OF FOUR FREEDOMS PLAZA, THE FANTASTIC FOUR.
"THE FEW SUPER-POWERED BEINGS REMAINING, INCLUDING THE ELUSIVE X-MEN, HAVE NOT MADE THEMSELVES AVAILABLE FOR QUESTIONING BY AUTHORITIES."
TERRIBLE. TERRIBLE. MAKES YOU WONDER WHY ANYONE WOULD PUT ON A COSTUME AND FIGHT CRIME AGAIN.
YEAH. SURE DOES.

"BUT NATURE **ABHORS** A VACUUM, AND THE DISAPPEARANCE OF THE HEROES HAS BROUGHT FORTH NEW DEFENDERS, SUCH AS THE **THUNDERBOLTS...**

"...AN AMBITIOUS GROUP WHO, IN THEIR EARLIEST PUBLICIZED CASE, TACKLED THE MOST **POWERFUL** SURVIVOR OF THE ONSLAUGHT DEBACLE... **THE INCREDIBLE HULK."**

OBSERVATION LOG OF PROFESSOR **WARREN ROTHSCHILD,** DAY 147. RECORDING.
IT'S BEEN A **WEEK** SINCE I HAD A TRULY GOOD NIGHT FOR OBSERVATION. IF THIS KEEPS UP...
...I MAY CHANGE MY VOCATION FROM **ASTRONOMER** TO **ARK BUILDER...**
Eh? NOW **THAT'S** IMPRESSIVE! WHATEVER IT IS, I WISH I COULD SEE IT **CLOSER!**
WAIT, IT'S... IT **IS** GETTING CLOSER. WHAT THE **DEVIL** IS --?

EEYAARGH!

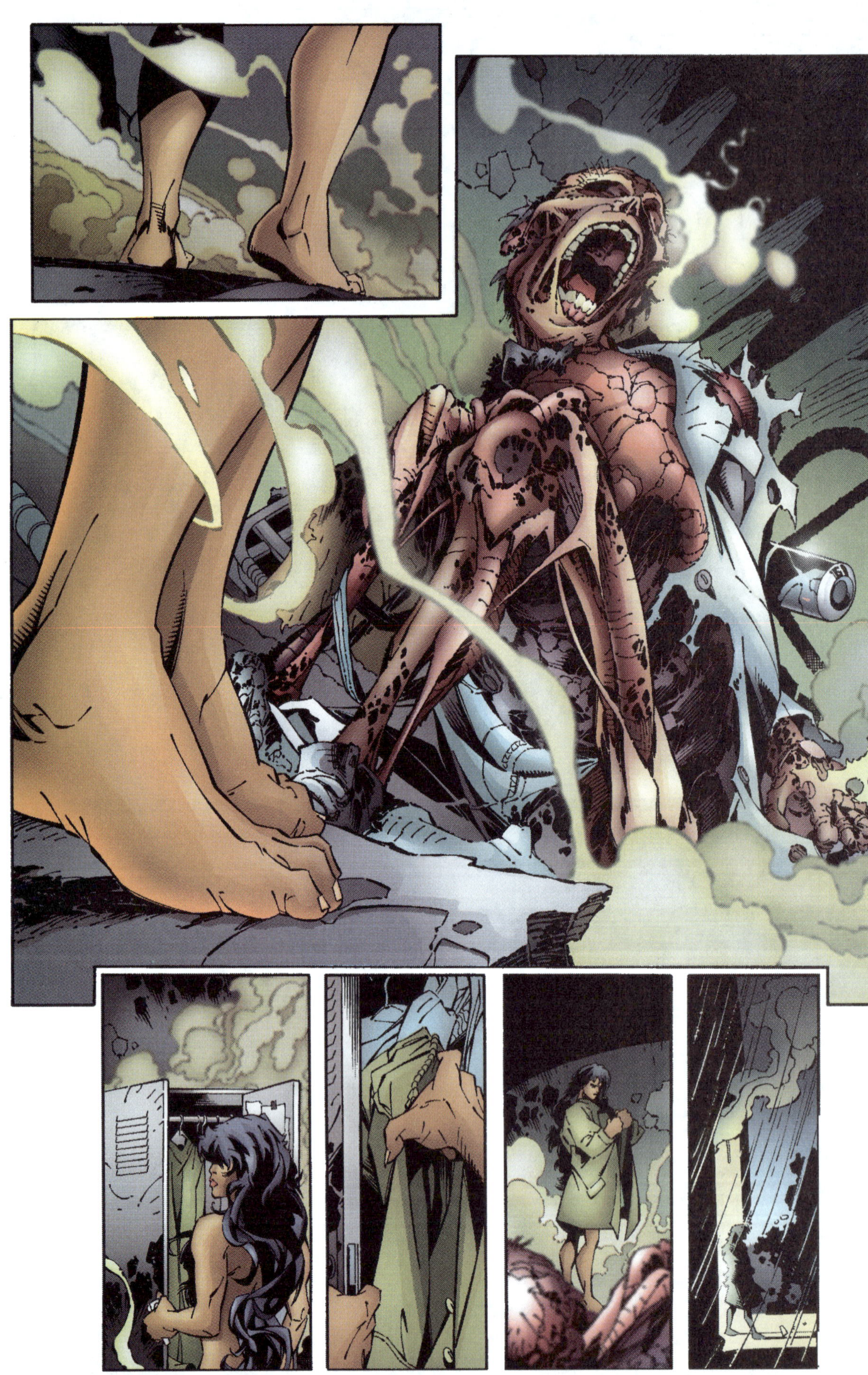

GIVE IT BACK --!
-- NOW!
NO! NOT THAT, TOO!
I WANT IT BACK!
THE MAN-THING HESITATES... FOR THE FEAR IS DISSIPATING...
...WASHED AWAY BY ANGER.
BUT THEN, THE FORCE OF THE BLUE BALL GENERATES TRANSFORMATIONS ALL ITS OWN.
AS ANGER BECOMES WONDER...
...WONDER BECOMES RAPTURE...
...AND PREDATOR... BECOMES LUGGAGE.
I KNEW I'D GET YOU BACK. I KNEW IT.

Oh. **HI.** SEE THE 'GATOR? HE BLOWED UP PRETTY **GOOD,** Huh?

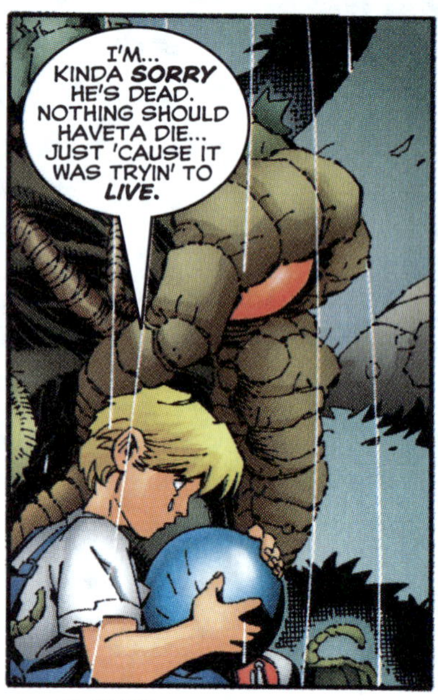
I'M... KINDA **SORRY** HE'S DEAD. NOTHING SHOULD HAVETA DIE... JUST 'CAUSE IT WAS TRYIN' TO **LIVE.**

BUT HE **SHOULDN'TA** TRIED TO EAT THIS. NOT **THIS.** IT'S... IT'S **'PORTANT.**

JUST... WISH I KNEW **WHY.**
GEE... THERE'S MOVIN' PICTURES IN MY **BALL.** IT'S NEVER DONE **THAT** BEFORE.

AND IN THE OTHER WORLD...
AND THE LORD SPOKE UNTO NOAH AND TOLD HIM HE WAS GOING TO DESTROY THE EARTH! AND NOAH OFFERED NO ARGUMENTS, BUT SIMPLY ACCEPTED THE LORD'S WORD AND SAVED HIMSELF!
AND SOME SCHOLARS FEEL NOAH WAS LESS THAN PIOUS, BECAUSE HE SHOULD HAVE TRIED TO ARGUE WITH GOD, OR TO SAVE HIS FELLOW MAN!
FOR AS JACOB WRESTLED WITH AN ANGEL, SO IT IS THE DESTINY OF MANKIND TO STRUGGLE WITH THE DIVINE...
MINE HEAD BE THROBBING AT THIS BATTLE, BUT THOR SHALL NOT CEASE UNTIL THE HULK CRIES, "HOLD, ENOW!"
THE THING AIN'T GIVING UP NEITHER, WINGHEAD... BECAUSE IT'S CLOBBERIN' TIME!
CHOOOM

UNCA... UNCA BEN?!

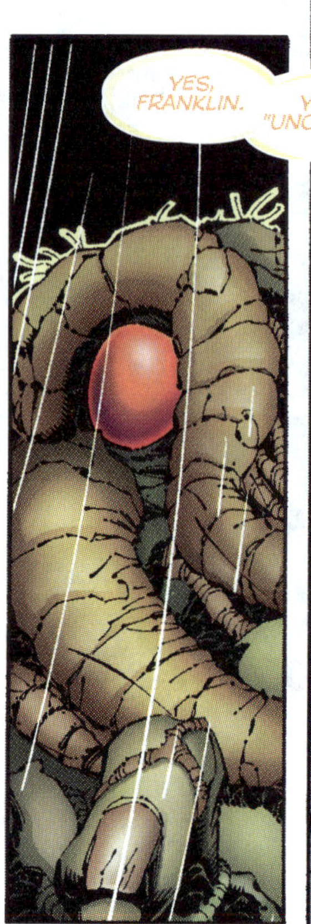
YES, FRANKLIN.
YOUR "UNCA BEN".

YOU ARE READY, AT LAST...
...TO SEE.

ONE SIDE, CREATURE. YOUR ATTEMPTS TO PROTECT FRANKLIN ARE NO LONGER NECESSARY...

...OR EVEN POSSIBLE.

LOOK INTO MY EYES, CREATURE...
...AND KNOW ME.
...FEAR
AND UPON KNOWING ME... KNOW...
FWOOOSH
WH -- WHAT DID YOU DO TO HIM?
NOTHING.
IT DID IT TO ITSELF.
I AM ASHEMA... SHE WHO HEARS...
...AND WE MUST TALK.

NEAR THE END OF A TYPICALLY ATYPICAL DAY FOR THE FANTASTIC FOUR...

AND THE GREEN-SKINNED CREEP GOT **AWAY!**

I'M... SURE IT WASN'T **YOUR** FAULT, BEN.

YEAH, IT **WAS,** SUZIE-Q. I WASN'T AT THE TOP OF MY GAME. IT WAS LIKE...

...LIKE SOMETHIN' WAS RATTLIN' AROUND IN MY HEAD. **DISTRACTIN'** ME.

I'M SURE YOU'LL SUCCEED **NEXT** TIME, BEN. I'M QUITE SURE.

HMMF. THIS TEA IS ICE-COLD.

HE'S NOT A "IT," HE'S A "HE," AND YOU BRING HIM BACK!
"HE" IS UNIMPORTANT.

HE'S ALIVE! THAT MAKES HIM 'PORTANT, IS WHAT MY MOMMY ALWAYS SAID!
LOWER YOUR VOICE.

I'LL SHOUT IF I WANNA SH--

LOWER YOUR VOICE

IS THIS BETTER?
YES.

FRANKLIN... I SHALL TRY TO EXPLAIN THIS IN A WAY YOU'LL UNDERSTAND.
WHAT DOES YOUR FATHER DO... WHEN HE HAS FINISHED AN EXPERIMENT?

Uh... WELL, HE SAYS SUMFIN' LIKE "I DID IT," AND THEN UNCA BEN MAKES FUN OF HIM...
...AND SOMETIMES STUFF BLOWS UP...

...AND THEN HE... CLEANS UP, I GUESS.
EXACTLY.
FRANKLIN... I AM PART OF A GREAT RACE OF BEINGS CALLED THE CELESTIALS. OUR TRUE FORMS WOULD LIKELY FRIGHTEN YOU, SO I HAVE CHOSEN THIS ONE.
WE CONDUCT EXPERIMENTS, TOO. AND ONE OF THEM WAS ON THIS WORLD, AS LIFE DEVELOPED.

BUT WE HAVE ACCOMPLISHED ALL WE SET OUT TO DO.
LIKE... LIKE WHAT?

TO MAKE YOU, FRANKLIN. OR SOMEONE LIKE YOU.
AND NOW IT'S TIME TO WIPE OFF THE PETRI DISH. TAKE THE EXPERIMENT'S RESULT AND CLEAN UP EVERYTHING ELSE.

YOU'RE... YOU'RE GONNA CLEAN OFF... EARTH?!
BUT... YOU CAN'T! I DON'T WANT YOU TO! IF YOU DO, I'LL...

YOU WILL DO AS YOU DID BEFORE.
YOU MUST SEE YOUR HANDIWORK... TO UNDERSTAND WHAT LIES BEFORE YOU.

HEEYYYYYYYY

MAKE THIS... STOP... I...
I WANT MY MOM... AND DAD... I WANT MY...

THEY ARE HERE.
YOU HAVE SENT THEM HERE... TO THIS WORLD.
BUT BUT THIS IS MY WORLD... MY HOME MY...

NO.

THIS IS ANOTHER WORLD. LOOK AROUND YOU. THIS IS HOW WE KNEW THAT HUMANITY HAD REACHED ITS PINNACLE IN YOU.

YOU HAVE CREATED... LIFE. YOU HAVE PRODUCED SOMETHING FROM NOTHING.
YOUR PARENTS, AS THEY EXIST HERE, ARE INDISTINGUISHABLE FROM THOSE AROUND YOU.

YOU HAVE CREATED GREATNESS IN THIS, YOUR OWN UNIVERSE, FRANKLIN.
YOU ARE, TO ALL INTENTS AND PURPOSES, GOD OF THIS UNIVERSE. BUT FOR YOU TO LEARN AND GROW -- TO UNDERSTAND YOUR OBLIGATIONS -- A SACRIFICE MUST BE MADE.
IF YOU DO NOT DESIRE THAT WE WIPE AWAY THE NO-LONGER NECESSARY EARTH... THEN YOU MUST OBLITERATE THIS WHICH YOU YOURSELF HAVE CREATED.
BUT IT'S... IT'S FULLA REAL PEOPLE! YOU SAID SO!
IF I 'CLEAN IT UP'... THEN WON'T THEY BE DEAD?
IT'D BE LIKE... LIKE I KILLED THEM. AND MOM AND DAD SAID KILLIN' IS REAL BAD!
I BELIEVE THE HUMANS HAVE PHRASED IT RATHER SUCCINCTLY.
THE LORD GIVETH... AND THE LORD TAKETH AWAY.
HERE -- ALLOW ME TO SHOW YOU WHAT YOU HAVE DONE.

I'M SO SORRY, REED... I DON'T KNOW WHAT CAME OVER ME TODAY.
IT WAS AS IF... I DON'T KNOW...
ALL SORTS OF PROBLEMS JUST... LANDED ON ME ALL AT ONCE...

MOMMY! DADDY! IT'S... IT'S REALLY YOU!
YOU'RE HERE! SHE WAS RIGHT! SHE -- I MEAN, THEY --

IT'S ME! IT'S FRANKLIN!
MOM! DAD! THEY... THEY TOLD ME I GOTTA WIPE OUT A UNIVERSE... AND I DON'T KNOW WHICH ONE..!
TELL ME WHICH ONE I SHOULD GET RIDDA...
...AND PROMISE YOU WON'T BE MAD AT ME..?
TO BE CONTINUED!

CHAPTER TWO
SECOND COMING

STAN LEE PRESENTS:
HEROES REBORN
THE RETURN PART 2 OF 4
MORTAL! "SORCERER SUPREME" WHO TRAVAILS UNDER THE APT NAME OF "DOCTOR STRANGE..." LABORING AWAY IN YOUR PRECIOUS SANCTUM WITH YOUR TRIVIAL "ORB OF AGAMOTTO..."
...CEASE SUCH TIME-WASTING FOOLISHNESS TO REFLECT NEW PRIORITIES. FOR LOKI ODINSON, THE TRICKSTER, HAS NEED OF THEE!
SECOND COMING
PETER DAVID WRITER
SALVADOR LARROCA PENCILER
ART THIBERT INKER
RICHARD STARKINGS & COMICRAFT/AD LETTERS
STEVE BUCCELLATO COLORS
POLLY WATSON ASS'T EDITOR
BOBBIE CHASE EDITOR
BOB HARRAS CHIEF

OF ALL WHO WALK YOUR PALTRY PLANET, I PERCEIVE ONLY YOU HAVE A GLIMMERING OF WHAT HAS TRULY HAPPENED! ONLY YOU KNOW THAT AN ALTERNATE UNIVERSE EXISTS... WITHIN WHICH MANY POWERFUL BEINGS ARE TRAPPED...
INCLUDING YOU, OLD ENEMY?
YOU NE'ER POSED SUFFICIENT THREAT TO CONSTITUTE AN ENEMY.
NOR AN ALLY, APPARENTLY... UNTIL NOW. BUT I'VE NO IDEA HOW TO RELEASE YOU, LOKI.
I SENSE THERE IS SOME MEANS OF ACCESS OTHER THAN THE FAIRLY VOLATILE ENERGIES POSSESSED BY THE HULK... BUT I CAN'T LOCATE IT.
HOWEVER... WHAT I HAVE LOCATED... IS YOU...
...IN THIS DIMENSION. SAFE, SOUND, AND MAKING TROUBLE.
CALUMNIES! ABSURDITY!
CLAIM YOU I BE A BASE IMPOSTOR?! FIE!
FIND A NEXUS POINT, STRANGE! FOR MY MAGIKS TELL ME THAT TIME GROWS SHORT!
MATTERS OF COSMIC CONSIDERATION CONVERGE UPON BOTH YOUR WORLDS!
MIGHT I SUGGEST ALLYING YOURSELF WITH THOR...
... PRESUMING HE'S THERE WITH YOU? OR WOULD DEATH BE A PREFERABLE ALTERNATIVE?
MAYHAP.

YOU *CANNOT!!*

BRA KOOM

GONE. NOT THAT HE WAS EVER *TRULY* HERE.

WHAT IN THE NAME OF THE VISHANTI COULD SO *ALARM* A *GOD?*

GREETINGS, GODLING. I AM ASHEMA OF THE CELESTIALS!
BEYOND THE EDGE OF SUBSPACE, TO THE CUSP OF ETERNITY, HAVE I BROUGHT YOU TO INFORM YOU THAT THIS BUSINESS IS NOT YOURS TO INTERFERE WITH.
OUR AFFAIRS ARE AS FAR ABOVE YOURS AS YOURS ARE ABOVE AN ANT'S.
AND WE DEAL WITH YOU... AS YOU WOULD AN ANT...
NOOOO!

AND THAT'S WHAT'S *HAPPENING*, MA! DAD! HONEST! I'M NOT LYING! I *NEVER* LIED TO YOU!
OKAY, OKAY, I BROKE THE COOKIE JAR!
COOKIE... JAR?
THAT TIME! THAT TIME I SAID I DIDN'T KNOW *WHO* BROKE THE COOKIE JAR, BUT UNCA BEN, HE SAID *HE* DID IT?

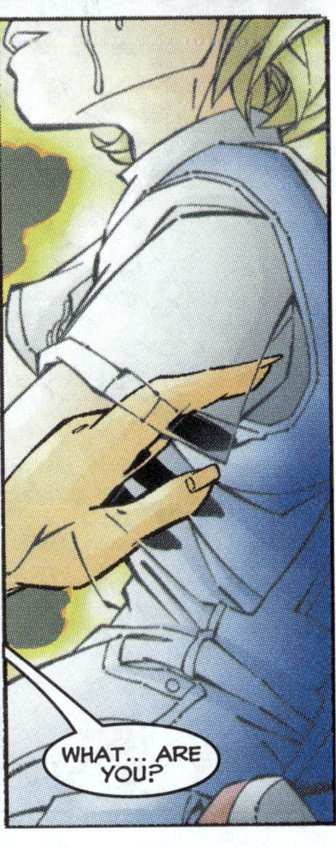

Y'GOTTA BELIEVE ME! THE CESTIALS ARE COMIN', AND I GOTTA MAKE A WHOLE WORLD GO 'WAY, AND I DUNNO WHICH ONE!
I MADE THIS WORLD TO SAVE YOU... I DUNNO HOW, BUT I DID! AND I GOTTA FIGGER OUT HOW TO SAVE EVERY-BODY B'FORE IT'S --!

FRANKLIN!
FRANKLIN!
SUSAN, CALM DOWN...

IT WAS HIM, REED! THE BOY I SAW IN THE NEGATIVE ZONE, WITH ME, EXCEPT IT WASN'T ME!
AND FRANKLIN WAS MY FATHER'S NAME! HE --!
SUE, LET'S BE REASONABLE. THIS --
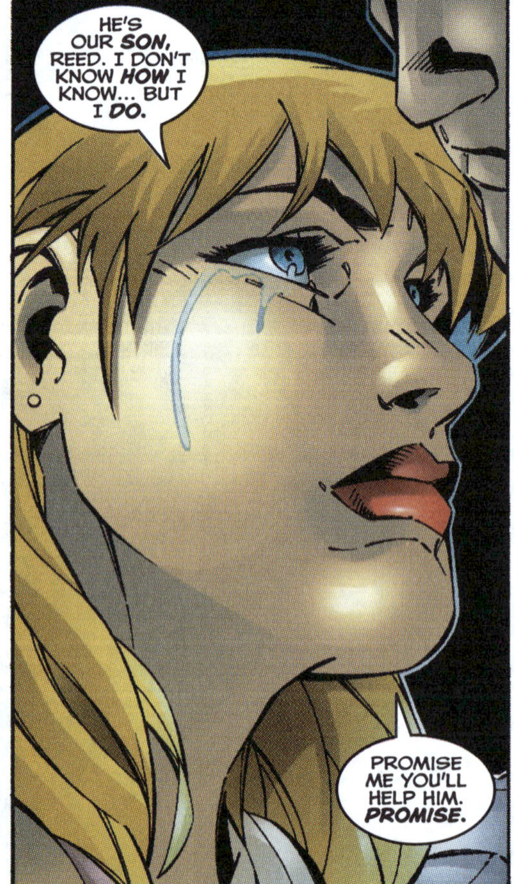
HE'S OUR SON, REED. I DON'T KNOW HOW I KNOW... BUT I DO.
PROMISE ME YOU'LL HELP HIM. PROMISE.

I PROMISE.

WHILE, A UNIVERSE AWAY, IN FOREST HILLS...
OOOYY...

I'M GOING STIR CRAZY. FEEL LIKE I SHOULD BE OUT DOING SOMETHING...
...INSTEAD OF SITTING HERE, STEWING INSIDE.
AND I FEEL LIKE... I'M NEEDED SOMEWHERE. JUST WISH I KNEW WHERE THAT WAS...

AND WHILE SUPER-POWERED CITIZENS PITCH IN ALL ACROSS THE COUNTRY TO DEAL WITH DISASTERS CAUSED BY THE COAST-TO-COAST TORRENTIAL RAINS...

...HERE IN MANHATTAN, REPORTS OF THE HULK'S PRESENCE HAVE LEFT CITIZENS ON EDGE... AND THERE ARE FEW "DEFENDERS" AVAILABLE TO DEAL WITH THIS MENACE.

Uh BOY.

BY THIS TIME TOMORROW, I'M GONNA BE SICK AS A DOG.

PRESUMING I'M LUCKY ENOUGH TO LIVE THAT LONG.

Jekyll AND HYDE

LIGHTS SHORT OUT AS HE PASSES.

DOESN'T REGISTER **AT ALL**.

ENERGY RAGES WITHIN HIM THAT HE **CANNOT** CONTROL.

HE HAS NEVER BEEN **STRONGER**...

...AND HE'S DYING.

HULK! YOU MUST SURRENDER!

NOW!

BUT GOING QUIETLY INTO THE GOOD NIGHT... IS **NOT** HIS STYLE.

BRUCE... COLONEL ST. LAWRENCE DOESN'T WANT TO HAVE TO ***FIRE*** ON YOU!

BUT YOU'RE SHORTING OUT ENERGY ALL ***OVER*** THE PLACE! YOU'RE GIVING OFF WAVES OF... OF ***POWER*** THAT WE CAN'T EVEN ***UNDERSTAND!***

YOU HAVE TO BE ***CONTAINED!*** YOU HAVE TO --!

PARK... REMEMBER THIS PARK...
...ALL STARTED HERE... FIGURES... COMES BACK AROUND.
HULK! 'TIS HERCULES, YOUR ERSTWHILE OPPONENT, WHO ADDRESSES YOU NOW!
I REGRET THAT YOU PERCEIVE YOURSELF PERSECUTED... EVEN BY SUCH A RELATIVELY MEAGER ASSEMBLAGE AS THIS --
Oh, ON BEHALF OF THE THUNDERBOLTS, THANKS A FREAKIN' LOT, HERC...
QUIET, ATLAS... OR I SHALL REQUEST THE GENUINE ATLAS HAVE WORDS WITH YOU.
NOW THEN... HULK...
YOU DON'T GET IT! NO ONE GETS IT!
NO ONE --

-- DEFEATS THE HULK!
THE OTHER UNIVERSE, THE OTHER HULK, YET STILL EARTH...
PERHAPS THOU WERE NOT SET FOR A REMATCH QUITE SO SOON... BUT I AM MORE THAN PREPARED.

PREPARED... TO DIE... THUNDER MAN?
READILY, FOR THE GOOD OF ALL, WOULD I SACRIFICE ALL.
BUT METHINKS 'TWILL NOT COME TO THAT --

-- Eh?!?
ODIN'S EYE! WHAT HAPPENSTANCE IS THIS?!

MAGMA, AS IF FROM THE FLAMING GULLET OF SURTUR HIMSELF!

HEELLLPP!!

CALMLY, MORTALS! THE WHIRLING POWER OF MJOLNIR WILL PROTECT THEE!
GONE. WHILST I SAVED INNOCENTS, THE HULK TOOK THE OPPORTUNITY TO DEPART.
A WISE, IF MONSTROUS, TACTIC.
AND NOW THE LAVA SUBSIDES, AS IF NOTHING HAD BEEN AMISS. 'TIS PASSING STRANGE...
...AND THE CLIME... IS SOMEWHAT HOTTER THAN MY NORTHERN UPBRINGING WOULD CONSIDER... COMFORTABLE.

MEANTIME, A UNIVERSE AWAY...
...A GLOWING BLUE BALL REMAINS NESTLED IN A SWAMP, ITS SECRETS REMAINING ITS OWN.

THAT IS, UNTIL THERE IS...

...TO ECHO THE THUNDER GOD OF ANOTHER WORLD...
...A PASSING STRANGE.

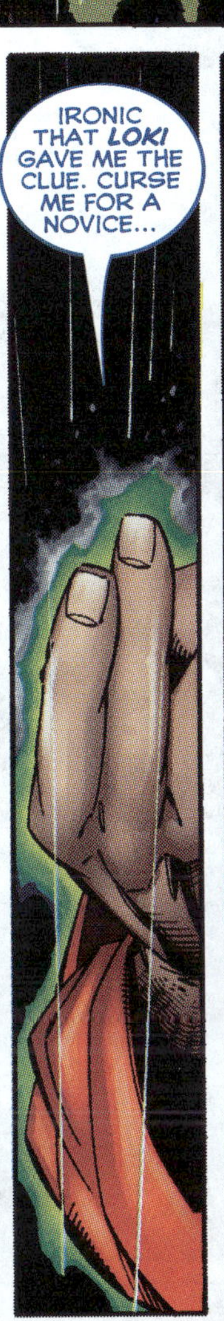
IRONIC THAT LOKI GAVE ME THE CLUE. CURSE ME FOR A NOVICE...

...I SHOULD HAVE THOUGHT TO MAKE THE NEXUS OF REALITIES ONE OF THE FIRST PLACES I WOULD SEARCH.
SO DISTRACTED WAS I BY THE ENERGIES SWIRLING ABOUT THE HULK...
...THAT IT DID NOT OCCUR TO ME TO RETURN TO BASICS.

IT WOULD BE INTERESTING TO BRING THIS... DEVICE... INTO THE HULK'S PRESENCE...

"...AND SEE THE RESULT."

WHILE, IN THE PLACE OF NO RAIN...
WHY DID YOU TAKE ME AWAY FROM MY MOMMY AND DADDY?! I NEED THEIR HELP --!
YOU DO NOT. YOU NEED ONLY YOURSELF TO MAKE THIS DETERMINATION. THE AID OF LESSER BEINGS...
THEY'RE NOT "LESSER BEANS," ASHEMA! THEY'RE MY MOM AND DAD, AND THIS IS MY PLACE, AND YOU WANT ME TO MAKE IT ALL GO 'WAY?
THIS OR THE WORLD OF YOUR BIRTH. BUT YOU MUST CHOOSE.
DO NOT BECOME CROSS WITH ME, FRANKLIN. THEREIN LIES GREAT DANGER.
WE CELESTIALS MAY BE INFINITE, BUT OUR PATIENCE IS NOT. AND WE ARE TAKING STEPS TO SOLVE THIS PROBLEM IF YOU DO NOT.
I'M GETTING TIRED OF YOU! YOU'RE MEAN AND YOU WANT ME TO MAKE EVER'BODY GO 'WAY! WELL, I WANT YOU TO GO 'WAY!

FRANK... LIN...
HEY, WHAT'S THAT?!
IT'S A CUB! A BEAR CUB!

HE MUSTA LOST HIS MOMMY IN THE JUNGLE!
SOMETHIN' HURT HIM, ASHEMA. SOME BIG ANIMAL MUSTA TRIED TO EAT HIM OR SOMETHIN'!

CAN YOU HELP HIM?
YOU CAN, IF YOU WISH.
I DUNNO HOW. YOU DO IT. PLEASE...

IT'S MERELY A CREATURE. IT MEANS NOTHING...

HE NEVER HURT ANYBODY! HE MEANS SOMETHIN' TO ME, AND IF I MEAN SOMETHIN' TO YOU, THEN HE SHOULD, TOO!

THERE. SATISFIED?

YOU DID IT! THANK YOU!

YOU'RE NOT SCARY AFTER ALL!

AND JUST LIKE THAT... THE BEAR IS GONE. SNUFFED OUT.

IT MEANS... NOTHING.
AND YOU... MUST CHOOSE... BEFORE IT'S TOO LATE.
I HATE YOU!
UNHH!
THAT WAS... UNEXPECTED...

Hmmm.
I DO *NOT* LIKE THE LOOKS OF THIS.

MEBBE. OR MEBBE IT'S 'CAUSE YOU WANTED *T' BELIEVE* YOU HAD A KID...
...EVEN IF IT MEANT THE WHOLE *WORLD* WAS COMIN' TO AN END BECAUSE OF THE *"CESTIALS."*

I... DON'T THINK THAT'S IT AT *ALL*.

WE HAVE A *PROBLEM.*
I'M TRACKING TWO FIREBALLS OF *UNKNOWN* ORIGINS --
-- AND THEY'RE ON A COLLISION COURSE WITH EARTH --
-- AND IT'S *GROWING.*
FURTHERMORE, I'VE RECORDED A TWO-DEGREE *INCREASE* IN WORLD-WIDE TEMPERATURE --
TO CAP IT OFF, THERE WAS A LAVA GEYSER IN MIDTOWN.
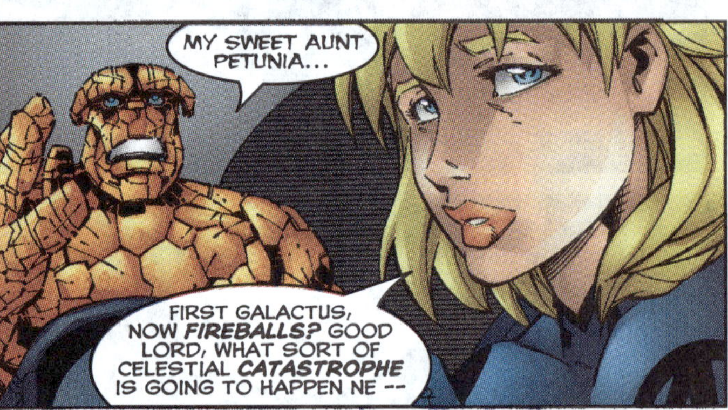
MY SWEET AUNT PETUNIA...
FIRST GALACTUS, NOW *FIREBALLS?* GOOD LORD, WHAT SORT OF CELESTIAL *CATASTROPHE* IS GOING TO HAPPEN NE --

CE... *LESTIAL?*
Oh, GOOD *LORD.*

NOT *"CESTIAL."* *"CELESTIAL."*
I'M CALLING *TONY* IN ON THIS... BEFORE IT'S TOO LATE.

CENTRAL PARK, A UNIVERSE AWAY...
...AS THE VERY ELEMENTS SEEM TO LEAD TO THE HULK'S UNCONSCIOUS COMMANDS.
A DOWNPOUR TRANSFORMS ITSELF INTO A DELUGE, TORRENTIAL WAVES DRIVING BACK THE HULK'S ATTACKS.
TOO LATE, DO YOU HEAR ME?!

TOO LATE TO SAVE ME... OR THE WORLD!
TOO LATE TO DO ANYTHING, EXCEPT LEAVE ME ALONE!
SO WHY WON'T YOU DO THE ONE THING YOU CAN... AND LEAVE!
WHILE, PERCHED IN A NEARBY TREE...
Aww, BROTHER...
...IT'S MOMENTS LIKE THIS I WISH I WAS JUST A CLONE.
WELL... NOW IT'S THE TIME TO SEE WHETHER THE ENERGIES OF THIS BALL ARE --
-- Eh?

HEY, HERCULES! SON OF A GOD --
--LOOKS LIKE, FOR ONCE, GOD'S ON MY SIDE!

HULK! YOU'VE GOTTA GET OUT OF HERE! GET SOMEWHERE SAFE, BEFORE YOU DESTROY THE WHOLE CITY JUST BY STANDING THERE!
GLUB SPIDER-MAN! BE GONE, WEBBED ONE! YOU'LL SERVE NO PURPOSE HERE!

Aw, GO HANG OUT WITH XENA OR SOMETHING!
HULK, LISTEN TO ME --!

NO! I'M THROUGH LISTENING! I DON'T HAVE TO LISTEN TO ANYONE! I'M...

...Huh?

WHOOAAA

THE CELESTIALS' ARRIVAL BRINGS MATTERS TO A CLIMAX, FRANKLIN!

AS THE COMING OF WHALES CREATES GREAT WAVES...

...SO DOES THE COMING OF THE CELESTIALS CREATE ENERGY WAVES WHICH THREATEN NOT ONLY YOUR WORLD OF BIRTH...

...BUT THE WORLD WHICH YOU BIRTHED.

IF YOU DO NOT CHOOSE, WE SHALL CHOOSE FOR YOU...

...AND THE CHOICE SHALL BE TO OBLITERATE --

NOW --!
FINALLY!
HULK WILL
SMASH!
TO BE CONTINUED!

Chapter Three
Third Dimension

SOMEWHERE, IN A JUNGLE...
HER NAME IS ASHEMA, AND SHE IS NOT ACCUSTOMED TO INCONVENIENCE... OR BEING DISCONCERTED...
...OR ANYTHING REFLECTING THE HUMAN CONDITION.

THE CHILD, FRANKLIN -- WHY IS HE MAKING SUCH A FUSS? WHY CAN HE NOT SIMPLY DECIDE WHICH IS TO BE OBLITERATED: HIS OWN WORLD, OR THE SPHERE WHICH HE CREATED?
SHE HAS SEEN LIFE IN BILLIONS OF DIFFERENT FORMS THROUGHOUT THE COSMOS. WHY DO THESE LITTLE EARTH PEOPLE SEEM COMPLETELY UNABLE TO DEAL WITH IT? WHY IS FRANKLIN BEING SUCH A NUISANCE?

AT LEAST HE STOPPED CRYING. HE WAS RUNNING, SHOUTING JUST UP AHEAD, AND THEN CEASED.
PERHAPS HE'S COME TO HIS SENSES. PERHAPS...

HMMF. A CLIFF.
FRANKLIN?
FRANKLIN?

CLEARLY HE BOLTED, UNSEEING, OFF THE EDGE OF THE PRECIPICE, TAKING A FALL OF AT LEAST A HUNDRED FEET. HE IS NOT MOVING. BARELY BREATHING.

AND ASHEMA LOOKS DOWN.
AND PONDERS THE SITUATION.

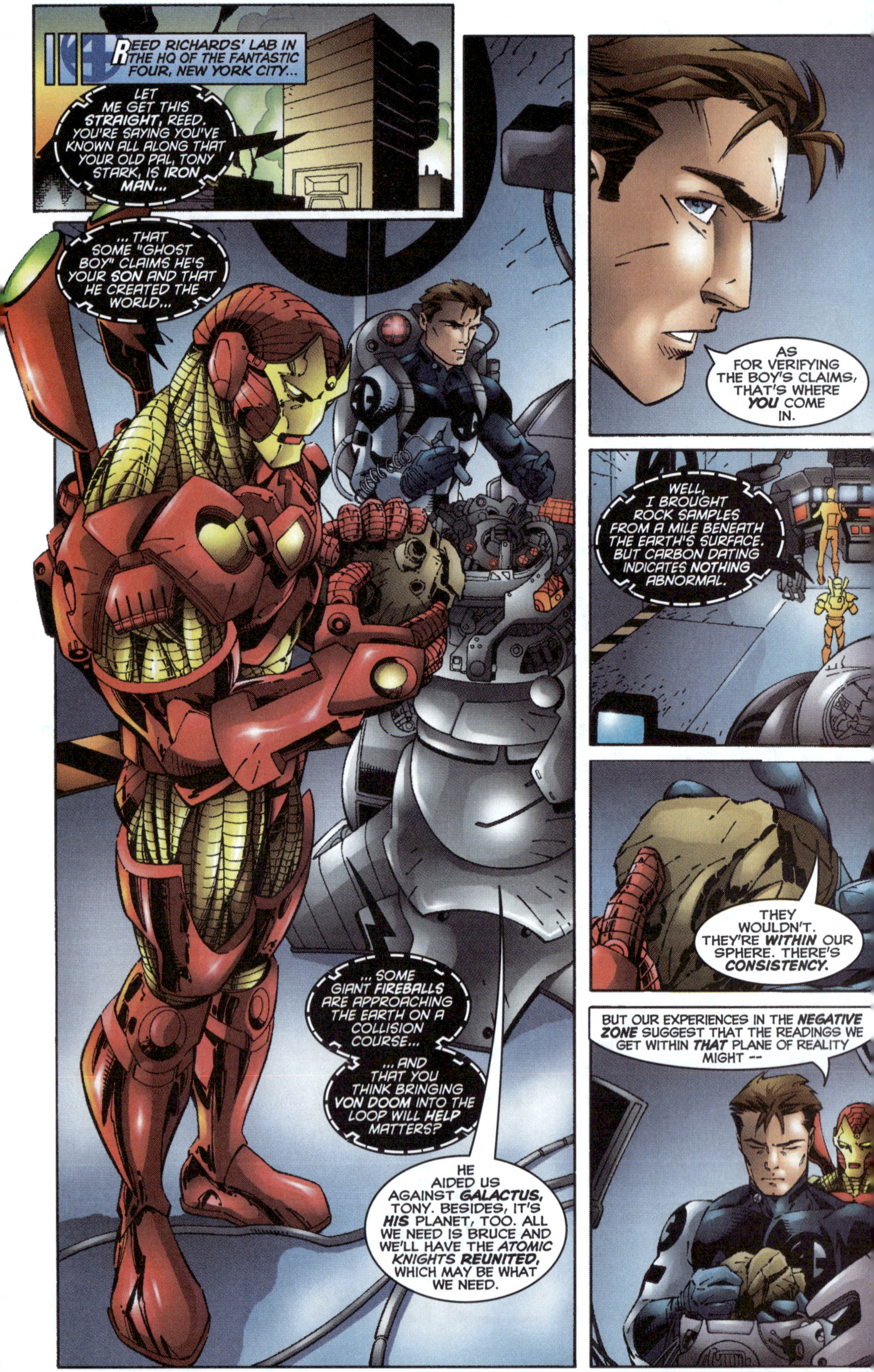

REED RICHARDS' LAB IN THE HQ OF THE FANTASTIC FOUR, NEW YORK CITY...

LET ME GET THIS **STRAIGHT**, REED. YOU'RE SAYING YOU'VE KNOWN ALL ALONG THAT YOUR OLD PAL, TONY STARK, IS **IRON MAN**...

...THAT SOME "GHOST BOY" CLAIMS HE'S YOUR **SON** AND THAT HE CREATED THE WORLD...

...SOME GIANT **FIREBALLS** ARE APPROACHING THE EARTH ON A COLLISION COURSE...

...AND THAT YOU THINK BRINGING **VON DOOM** INTO THE LOOP WILL **HELP** MATTERS?

HE AIDED US AGAINST **GALACTUS**, TONY. BESIDES, IT'S **HIS** PLANET, TOO. ALL WE NEED IS BRUCE AND WE'LL HAVE THE **ATOMIC KNIGHTS REUNITED**, WHICH MAY BE WHAT WE NEED.

THE FIREBALLS I'M TRACKING HAVE PICKED UP SPEED. AT THIS POINT, I'D GAUGE THEIR ARRIVAL IN FOUR DAYS... PERHAPS **SOONER.**
SWELL... OKAY, REED, AS WE **DISCUSSED...** YOU MONITOR FROM HERE, AND I'LL TAKE THE ROCKS INTO THE NEGATIVE ZONE AND RUN THE **TESTS.** LET'S **DO** IT.

VON DOOM AND BRUCE BANNER, POTENTIAL **ALLIES** AGAIN.
THIS THING JUST GETS WILDER AND **WILDER.**

STUPID FAKE HULK THINKS HE CAN FOOL HULK! BUT NO ONE FOOLS HULK!

STAN LEE PRESENTS:
HEROES REBORN
THE RETURN PART 3 OF 4
GUYS, WAIT! HOLD IT! THIS WON'T ACCOMPLISH ANYTHING!
BANNER! I'D RECOGNIZE YOU... ANYWHERE!
BEEN... LOOKING FOR YOU... AND NOW THAT I'VE FOUND YOU...
...I'LL SMASH YOU!
THIRD DIMENSION
PETER DAVID WRITER
SALVADOR LARROCA PENCILER
THIBERT/LAROSA PEPOY/PRUDEAUX INKERS
RICHARD STARKINGS & COMICRAFT/KF LETTERS
STEVE BUCCELLATO COLORS
POLLY WATSON ASS'T EDITOR
BOBBIE CHASE EDITOR
BOB HARRAS CHIEF

GOOD LORD... I'M STANDING BETWEEN TWO HULKS...
...WHAT AM I, NUTS?!

CRIPES, **HOW** DID WE WIND UP ON THE GEORGE WASHINGTON BRIDGE?!

AND THE RAIN... THE RAIN'S **STOPPED!** INSTEAD IT'S SO... SO **HOT** THAT IT'S ALMOST **SUFFOCATING!**

AND WHERE DID THAT **SECOND** HULK COME FROM? OR MAYBE THE **BETTER** QUESTION IS...

...WHERE DID **WE** COME FROM?

BECAUSE HULK IS THE STRONGEST ONE THERE IS!

YOU... THIS IS...
...THIS IS ALL... YOUR FAULT...
...YOU LEFT ME... BETRAYED ME...

THIS IS ALL YOUR FAULT!

MAYBE I'D BETTER GET TO A SAFE DISTANCE...
...LIKE PERU.
YOU THINK... BECAUSE YOU'RE BANNER... YOU'RE THE REAL HULK..?

EVER SINCE LOSING BANNER... I'VE BEEN SEARCHING... FOR COMPLETION...
...SEARCHING FOR MORE THAN I WAS... LIKE A CRIPPLE... NEEDING A CRUTCH...
...AND NOW THAT I'VE FOUND YOU... AND SEEN YOU... AND REMEMBER WHAT IT WAS LIKE... HAVING YOU IN MY HEAD...
...I KNOW NOW...
...YOU'RE OUT OF MY MIND! AND I LIKE IT THAT WAY!

IF THE TWO HULKS ARE AWARE THAT THEY HAVE GONE OVER THE EDGE OF THE BRIDGE, THEY DON'T ACKNOWLEDGE IT.

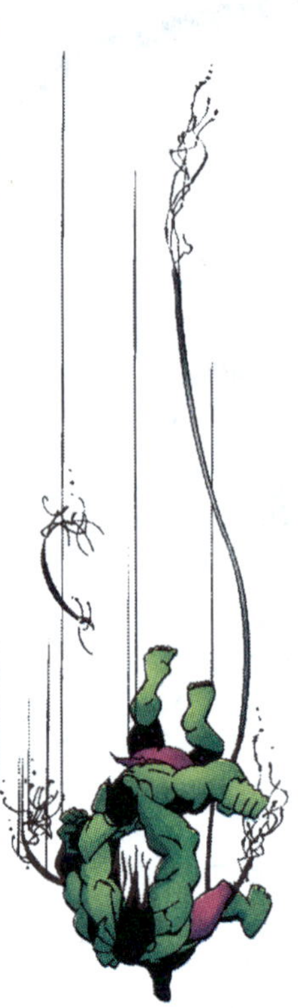
INSTEAD, AS THE LARGER HULK SNAPS THE CABLE, THEY PROCEED TO TRY AND THROTTLE EACH OTHER.

AND DO SO ALL THE WAY UNTIL THEY DISAPPEAR BENEATH THE RIVER SURFACE.

AW, TERRIFIC. AND ME WITHOUT MY FLOATIES.

ALL RIGHT... WHERE IS HE? WHERE IS THE HULK?
AND WHO ARE YOU?!

Oh... MY GOD! YOU'RE ALIVE!

BACK IN THE JUNGLE...
WITH ALL THE WISDOM OF THE CELESTIALS... WE STILL NEVER EXPECTED SUCH AN ODD ENDING TO THE EXPERIMENT.
VARIED AND UNEXPECTED ARE THE PATHS OF DISCOVERY.
YOU WILL BE AT PEACE, FRANKLIN. PASS ON.
WHAT?
SAVE HIM? BUT...
BUT HE HAS PROVEN SO... SO INADEQUATE. SO FRAGILE. WHAT IS THE POINT OF --?
OHHH... VERY WELL. FRANKLIN, IT SEEMS I AM TO SAVE...
...YOU?
THE END HAS COME UPON HIM... THE DEATH RATTLE IN HIS THROAT... AND SHE REACHES OUT... REACHES WITH CELESTIAL ABILITY...
...AND CATCHES THE EPHEMERAL THING CALLED THE HUMAN SOUL, AS SHE ATTEMPTS TO REJOIN IT TO HIS BODY WITH AN INSTINCT SHE DIDN'T KNOW SHE POSSESSED.
AND IN TOUCHING HIS SOUL...

...SHE TOUCHES THE SOUL OF EVERYONE IN THE WORLD.
FOR THIS WORLD ORIGINATED WITH FRANKLIN. BY BONDING WITH HIS SOUL, HE CONNECTS WITH EVERY LIVING CREATURE ON THE FACE OF THIS EARTH.
SUCH A CRASH COURSE IN HUMANITY IS HUMBLING, NUMBING... EVEN FOR A CELESTIAL IN HUMAN FORM.
FOR ASHEMA, WHO HAS SPENT ETERNITY BEING ABOVE IT ALL, HAS SUDDENLY FOUND HERSELF OVER HER HEAD IN HUMAN EXPERIENCE. AS IF SHE WERE REMEMBERING THINGS SHE DID NOT KNOW SHE'D FORGOTTEN.

AH...
...A...
ASHEMA..?
ARE YOU...
CRYING?
NO...
NO, I AM NOT...
ABSOLUTELY...
NOT...
CAN...
CAN I GO...
TO MY MOM
AND DAD
NOW?
YES.

MEANWHILE, IN NEW YORK...

...THE TWO HULKS STRUGGLE **FURIOUSLY**, TRYING TO CHOKE THE LIFE FROM ONE ANOTHER... TO, BASICALLY, **DROWN** EACH OTHER.

IT IS VERY LIKELY THAT **BOTH** WILL DIE...

IT'S... IT'S NOT POSSIBLE.
WHAT HAPPENED, IRON MAN? WHAT DID THE READINGS IN THE ZONE SAY?
ACCORDING TO THESE... THIS SAMPLE FROM OUR SUBSTRATA, FROM OUR WORLD...

...IS LESS THAN A YEAR OLD.
GOD IN HEAVEN.

WE'VE GOT TO FIND FRANKLIN. HE'S THE ONLY ANSWER. AND HE SAID SOMETHING WAS COMING... THE CELESTIALS... AND A DECISION HAD TO BE MADE ABOUT EARTH LIVING OR DYING...

BZZT
BZZT

AS IF WE NEEDED SOMETHING ELSE TO EXACERBATE OUR SITUATION: THE FIRE-BALLS HAVE PICKED UP SPEED. E.T.A. TWENTY-EIGHT HOURS.
SUSAN IS RIGHT. WE HAVE TO FIND THE BOY, IMMEDIATELY...

DAD..? MOMMY..?

MOMMY!

ACROSS TOWN...
HEY, BUG-BOY! DO YOU HAVE ANYTHING TO DO WITH... THAT?!
IT'S "SPIDER-MAN," AND NO! I WAS HOPING YOU KNEW WHAT IT WAS!
I'M STILL TRYING TO ADJUST TO THE FACT THAT YOU GUYS ARE STILL SUCKING AIR!
HOLY MOTHER OF --!
WELL, DEAL WITH IT AND LET'S MOVE ON.
INCREDIBLE. IT JUST... JUST ROSE OUT OF THE RIVER LIKE...
BANNER! IT'S GOT BANNER IN SOME SORT OF FORCE BUBBLE... AND THAT OTHER HULK, TOO!

ATTENTION, THOSE OF YOU IN PURSUIT OF THIS VESSEL... AND REED RICHARDS, WHO I ASSUME IS MONITORING THIS BROADCAST, I PERCEIVE YOU HAVE SOME DIFFICULTIES TO BE ATTENDED TO.
RICHARDS HAS PROPOSED A REUNION OF OUR FORMER "CLIQUE," AND I HAVE TAKEN THE LIBERTY OF RETRIEVING BANNER...
...FOR THAT VERY PURPOSE.

IN CASE YOU ARE AT ALL INTERESTED, THIS "OTHER HULK" APPEARS TO BE "LEAKING" SOME SORT OF TRANSDIMENSIONAL ENERGY. MY FORCE DAMPENING BUBBLE HAS MANAGED TO KEEP IT IN CHECK SO THAT IT HAS NO HARMFUL EFFECT UPON THIS VESSEL.
IN THE EVENT THAT YOU ANTICIPATE AN ATTEMPT AT FLEEING ON MY PART...
...I WILL INFORM YOU THAT I AM HEADING STRAIGHTAWAY TO THE HEADQUARTERS OF THE FANTASTIC FOUR... THERE TO MEET WITH THE CLOSEST THAT I HAVE TO A PEER ON THIS PLANET. I SHALL NOT DEVIATE FROM THAT COURSE.
YOU HAVE THE WORD... OF DOCTOR DOOM.

THE STREETS OF MANHATTAN...
...WHERE THE SWELTERING HEAT... AND THE OVERALL SENSE OF IMPENDING DOOM...

...HAS CAUSED SOME TO GIVE FREE REIN TO THEIR GREED.
BUT AS THERE ARE SOME WHO FACE ARMAGEDDON WITH DARKNESS IN THEIR SOULS...

...THERE ARE OTHERS...

...WHO, TO THE END... FIGHT FOR THE LIGHT.
FALCON, I SURE WISH I KNEW WHERE CAP WAS!

YOU AND ME BOTH, BUCKY. YOU AND ME --

HOLY --!
IN THE SKY --! THOSE... THOSE FIREBALLS! AND THERE'S... THERE'S SOMETHING... FORMING AROUND THEM --! IT... I DON'T...

REED'S LAB...
YOU JUST HAPPENED TO HAVE A SPACE SHIP HANDY, DOOM?

THE WORLD NEARLY MET ITS END AT THE HANDS OF GALACTUS, IRON MAN. I WOULD BE MOST FOOLISH NOT TO HAVE AN ESCAPE VESSEL HANDY SHOULD SUCH A SCENARIO RECUR. ABOVE ALL, DOOM MUST SURVIVE.
AND WHEN RICHARDS APPRISED ME OF THE SITUATION WE FACE... I FELT IT MIGHT BE A USEFUL DEVICE TO HAVE CLOSE AT HAND, PRESUMING YOU ONCE AGAIN NEED MY AID.

SINCE BANNER WAS REQUIRED, I TERMINATED THAT IMBROGLIO AS WELL.
SO, RICHARDS... YOU HAVE THE FLOOR. PERHAPS YOU'D BEST PROCEED.

PEOPLE, THE FOLLOWING EVIDENCE CANNOT BE IGNORED: THE AGE OF OUR WORLD, THE APPROACHING FIREBALLS -- THIS BOY'S -- I MEAN, MY "SON'S" STORY OF ANOTHER WORLD, VERIFIED BY THIS OTHER HULK AND "SPIDER-MAN..."
I KNOW IT SOUNDS INSANE, BUT --

IT'S WAY BEYOND INSANE, RICHARDS. NEXT STOP'S THE TWILIGHT ZONE.
WHAT DO YOU SUGGEST WE DO NEXT? PILE INTO DOOM'S SHIP AND HEAD BACK THERE?

ACTUALLY, HAWKEYE, I THINK THAT'S EXACTLY WHAT HE'S GOING TO PROPOSE.

YOU HAVE NO CHOICE.
AND WHO'S THIS AGAIN?
BE QUIET.
THE CELESTIALS HAVE GIVEN FRANKLIN AN ULTIMATUM, TO DETERMINE WHICH WORLD LIVES AND DIES. AND FRANKLIN... YOU'VE DECIDED, HAVEN'T YOU?

I'M... I'M SORRY, MA. I... CAN'T LET THE OTHER ONE GET BLOWED UP.
I MADE THIS ONE, AND I WISH I COULDA SAVED IT, BUT I DUNNO HOW AND I GOTTA CHOOSE...

THERE MUST BE A WAY TO SAVE BOTH. THERE IS, ISN'T THERE? SOMETHING YOU'RE NOT SAYING...

NO. AND YOUR ONLY HOPE IS ESCAPE. ALL OF YOU, TOGETHER. FOR YOUR TIME IS RUNNING OUT. THOSE "FIREBALLS" ARE MORE THAN THEY APPEAR --

WAIT... FROM THE STREETS BELOW... DO YOU HEAR IT..?

SCREAMING... PANIC. WHAT'S GOING ON?
Oh... MY LORD...

"I ASSUME YOU ARE CONVINCED?"

CHAPTER FOUR
FOURTH AND GOAL

STAN LEE PRESENTS:
HEROES REBORN
THE RETURN PART 4 OF 4
FOURTH & GOAL
IN ANOTHER UNIVERSE THAT MIRRORS OUR OWN...
IT HAS TAKEN CAJOLING... AND EXPLAINING... AND DEMONSTRATIONS...
...MUCH POINTING TO THE SKY, MUCH EFFORT, MUCH FAST TALKING, MUCH CALLING IN OF FAVORS, CASHING IN OF CHIPS, GENTLE AND LESS GENTLE PERSUASION...
YEAH... YEAH, I THINK THAT'S EVERYBODY...
YOU THINK THAT'S EVERYBODY?
Oh, I'VE GOT A BAD FEELING ABOUT THIS.
...IN SHORT, IT MAY BE THE SINGLE GREATEST EFFORT EXERTED SINCE THE CREATION OF THE WORLD.
THE GOAL? THE POSSIBLE SALVATION OF SAME.
PETER DAVID WRITER
SALVADOR LARROCA PENCILER
SCOTT HANNA INKER
RICHARD STARKINGS & COMICRAFT/KF LETTERS
STEVE BUCCELLATO COLORS
POLLY WATSON ASS'T EDITOR
BOBBIE CHASE EDITOR
BOB HARRAS CHIEF

THE BAXTER BUILDING, NEW YORK CITY -- IN THE LAB OF SCIENTIST REED RICHARDS...

YOU'RE THE MAN OF THE **HOUR**, VICTOR VON DOOM. ALL THOSE PEOPLE ON THE ROOF WOULDN'T HAVE A **PRAYER** IF YOU HADN'T PREPARED AN ESCAPE VESSEL.

NO GOOD DEED GOES UNPUNISHED. IS THAT NOT THE **SAYING,** RICHARDS?

FROM **MY** UNDERSTANDING, THE WORLD THAT AWAITS ME IS A PALE **SHADE** COMPARED TO WHAT I HAVE HERE.

THERE IS NO ALLURE TO DEPARTING THIS ONE... AND YET IT SEEMS INEVITABLE. MANDATORY.

WHAT OF **YOU,** TONY STARK? IS IT NOT **GALLING** TO HURL YOURSELF INTO THE UNKNOWN...

...WHEN YOU HAVE ALL A MAN COULD **WISH** FOR?

YES. BUT... IT WOULD SEEM THE **ONLY** WAY, RIGHT, BRUCE?

YES, IT WOULD. BUT PERHAPS WE NEED NOT DISSOLVE **OUR** ALLIANCE IN THE NEW... OLD... WORLD.

PERHAPS WE CAN **PRESERVE** WHAT WE HAVE HERE. AND IF WE CAN'T, FOR WHATEVER REASON...

...THEN AT LEAST THE ATOMIC KNIGHTS WENT OUT IN **STYLE,** SAVING A WORLD.

ON A ROOFTOP ACROSS TOWN...

YOU... YOU GOTTA BE *KIDDING!*

YOU'RE JUST... LEAVING ME *BEHIND?* YOU'RE GOING SOMEWHERE, TAKING FALCON AND NOT *ME?* THIS *BITES!*

THERE ARE WEIRD FLAMING EYES IN THE SKY, EVERYBODY'S TALKIN' *DOOMSDAY*... AND YOU AND BIRDBRAIN ARE OFF ON A SECRET MISSION? CAP, PLEASE, WHY CAN'T I *COME?!*

THE ANSWERS RACE THROUGH HIS MIND: "BECAUSE SAM AND I *AREN'T* FROM THIS WORLD... BECAUSE YOU'RE... A MANIFESTATION OF A YOUNG BOY'S *IMAGINATION*, MADE *MANIFEST* BY AN INCOMPREHENSIBLE POWER."

BACK AT F.F H.Q.
I SEE CAP AND THE FALCON. THEY'RE ON THEIR WAY...

GOOD. THAT WILL ACCOUNT FOR EVERYONE -- SUE?
YES.
BUT NOW... ASHEMA... I THINK IT IMPORTANT WE INFORM YOU...

...THAT WE'RE NOT JUST UP-AND-LEAVING AS EASILY AS THAT.

IMPOSSIBLE. FRANKLIN HAS CHOSEN THIS WORLD FOR OBLITERATION. AS ONE GROUP YOU ARRIVED IN THIS WORLD FROM YOUR OWN, AND AS ONE GROUP YOU MUST DEPART. AND NOW. OTHERWISE THE CELESTIALS WILL OBLITERATE BOTH WORLDS.
ONCE YOU'VE RETURNED, FRANKLIN WILL THEN COME WITH ME TO MEET HIS TRUE DESTINY.

I CAN REMOVE HIM FROM YOUR MEMORIES, IF YOU WISH, TO EASE THE STING OF DEPARTURE...
NO! I WON'T LET YOU --

NONE OF US WILL. REED RICHARDS SPEAKS FOR US ALL.
THIS WORLD -- "FICTION" OR NOT -- MUST BE PRESERVED. AND THE BOY WILL STAY WITH HIS PARENTS! SO SAY WE ALL.

NEVER HAVE THE HEROES BEEN AS CLOSE TO DEATH AS THEY ARE AT THIS MOMENT.

YOU ARE MY **LAST** HOPE. THE LAST HOPE OF **ALL OF** US. I HAVE APPROACHED YOU IN TIMES PAST, AND YOU HAVE **REFUSED** TO HELP -- EVEN THOUGH **I** HAVE **AIDED** YOU.

A BEING SUCH AS YOURSELF IS **ABOVE** NOTIONS OF GRATITUDE... BUT I AM **NOT.** WHATEVER YOU CAN DO... IF **ANYTHING...** PLEASE... GRANT ME THAT... BEFORE IT'S **TOO** LATE.

WE SHALL... CONSIDER IT. HOWEVER... LEAVE US THE GLOBE...

YOU... YOU MICROBES WITH PRETENSIONS OF SIGNIFICANCE!
I AM A CELESTIAL! I COULD OBLITERATE YOU WITH A THOUGHT, AND YOU DEFY ME?!

I COULD...

AND HE LOOKS AT HER... JUST... LOOKS AT HER...
...AND IN HIS EYES... AND IN THE EYES OF HER PEERS... FOR THE FIRST TIME IN HER ENDLESS EXISTENCE...

...ASHEMA FEELS...
...SMALL.

VERY WELL.
IF ALL OF YOU... WITH YOUR DISPARATE PERSONALITIES... CAN COME TOGETHER FOR A GREATER PURPOSE... THEN I WILL HONOR THAT. GO... AND THIS WORLD WILL LIVE ON.
YOU HAVE MY WORD.

THY WORD. AND WHAT REASON DO WE HAVE TO TRUST THAT?
I HAVE NO PURPOSE IN LYING.
PERHAPS. OR PERHAPS YOU FEAR OUR POWER AND WRATH!
SNAP
OR... PERHAPS NOT.
YOU WILL ALL LEAVE. NONE MUST REMAIN IN THIS SPHERE, OR ALL WILL PERISH. THOSE ARE THE TERMS. UNDERSTOOD?
GOOD.
BY THE WAY, WHERE'D TONY GO?
SOME LAST MINUTE BUSINESS, HE SAID.

TONY...

...DO YOU HAVE ANY IDEA HOW **GREAT** THAT WAS? AFTER ALL THIS TIME, I STILL --
-- TONY **WHY** ARE YOU --?

-- WHY ARE YOU WEARING THE **IRON MAN** COSTUME? AND WHY DO YOU LOOK... SO **SAD?**

I'M... **NOT.** I'M JUST THINKING ABOUT WHAT A... NICE APARTMENT YOU HAVE HERE, AND I...
...AND THERE'S THINGS I WANTED TO SAY... BUT THIS ISN'T HOW I **INTENDED** TO...
TO SAY **WHAT?** THAT YOU LOVE ME?

YES.

TAKE CARE, PEPPER.

Uhm... Uh... YOU TOO.
SEE YOU **LATER,** RIGHT?
RIGHT?

A COMING DISASTER BROUGHT ON BY GOD-LIKE BEINGS, AND AN ESCAPE IN A MASSIVE ARK. DOES ANY OF THIS SEEM FAMILIAR TO YOU, SPIDER-MAN?
I GUESS YOU COULD SAY THERE'S NOAH ACCOUNTING FOR TASTE, SHE-HULK.
AW GAWD. I WANNA SIT NEXT TO SOMEBODY ELSE.

WOW! THIS SHIP HAS EVERYTHING! COOL!
SURVIVAL ALONE IS INSUFFICIENT, LAD. ONE MUST SURVIVE...
...IN STYLE.

ASHEMA CONFIRMED THAT THE WAY HOME IS THROUGH THE NEGATIVE ZONE. IT'S NOT INFINITE -- THE OUTER BORDERS ARE, QUITE LITERALLY, THE BOUNDARIES OF FRANKLIN'S IMAGINATION.
IF WE CAN CROSS THAT "BORDER," WE CAN MAKE IT BACK. PROBLEM IS, THIS SHIP IS TOO BIG TO GET THROUGH THE PORTAL.

BUT RICHARDS AND I HAVE INCORPORATED SHRINKING TECHNOLOGY THAT HE WAS DEVELOPING TO EXPLORE AN AREA HE CALLS THE "MICROVERSE."

ALTHOUGH THE CHILD MIGHT HAVE BEEN ABLE TO SHRINK US HIMSELF. IMAGINE SUCH POWER... IN ONE SO YOUNG.

COME, GENTLEMEN. IT'S TIME. AND I HAVE TOO LITTLE TASTE FOR FLIES TO DESIRE THE TEMPTING OF FATE.
I KNOW, THOR. BUT I DISLIKE EVEN THE APPEARANCE OF RETREATING.
UNDERSTOOD, CAPTAIN. BUT IN MANY WAYS, WE ARE BUT SOLDIERS. AND WE DO WHAT MUST BE DONE...
...FOR THE BETTERMENT OF ALL.
VRRRRRR

HEY, WATCH IT!
IF YOU TOUCH ONE CONTROL, GRIMM, YOU WILL NOT LIVE TO SEE HOME AGAIN.
LIFT-OFF HAS BEEN ACHIEVED.
ENGAGE SIZE REDUCTION SYSTEMS.
YOU BIG BRAINS NEED A REAL PILOT UP THERE OR WHAT?!
YOU MEAN WE ALL HAVE TO GO ON WEIGHT WATCHERS?!
JEEZ, SPIDER-MAN, DO YOU EVER SHUT UP?!
YOU USED TO THINK I WAS FUNNY BACK WHEN WE WERE LOVERS, SHE-HULK.
THAT'S ANOTHER JOKE, RIGHT? TELL ME THAT'S A JOKE.
SORRY. TOO BUSY SHUTTING UP.

I SEE ASHEMA! SHE'S STANDING NEXT TO THE NEGATIVE ZONE DOOR!
HEY DAD! MOM! SHE --
-- SHE SMILED AT ME!
AND THEN, WITH A ROAR OF NEGATIVE SOLAR WINDS...
...THEY'RE GONE.

FOOLS. THEY HAVE SOWN THE SEEDS OF THEIR OWN DESTRUCTION...
...AND STILL THEY DO NOT UNDERSTAND!
WHY CAN THEY NOT SEE...
...THE LIGHT!

THREE MINUTES TO THE **BOUNDARY** AREA. IT'S AT THAT POINT THAT OUR **PREVIOUS** EXPEDITION WENT **AWRY.**
THIS TIME WE **HAVE** TO BREAK THROUGH, BECAUSE -- AT LEAST IN **THIS** REALITY -- THAT POINT FORMS THE **BORDER** BETWEEN OUR **WORLD**... AND OUR **HOME.**

YOUR SON SEEMS MOST **INTERESTED** IN MY VESSEL'S **WORKINGS.** HE HAS YOUR **EAGER** MIND, RICHARDS.
THANK YOU, VICTOR.

...AND WHAT DOOM ENVIES... DOOM MUST HAVE!
VON DOOM! LET HIM GO! HAVE YOU LOST YOUR MIND?!
I WOULD NOT HURT A CHILD FOR ALL THE WORLD. BUT FOR ALL THE UNIVERSE, WELL...
...COMPROMISES CAN AND MUST BE MADE!
FRANKLIN!
REED! WHAT'S HAPPENING?

WITHIN SECONDS, THE OTHERS -- ALERTED TO THE **EMERGENCY** -- CHARGE TOWARDS THE FRONT SECTION OF THE ARK.

BUT BE IT **SEVERAL** SECONDS OR EVEN **ONE**... IT MAKES **NO** DIFFERENCE...

...FOR THE EMERGENCY EXIT TUBE HAS ALREADY HURLED DOOM AND FRANKLIN INTO THE **VOID**.

YOU HEARD **ASHEMA!** WE GOTTA LEAVE THE SAME WAY WE ARRIVED -- **TOGETHER!** OR... OR THE CELESTIALS ARE GONNA WRECK **EVERYTHING!**

IF YOUR POWER IS **PROPERLY** HARNESSED, **I** CAN ATTEND TO THE CELESTIALS. AND EVEN NOW YOUR POWER IS FLOWING INTO **ME** VIA MY ARMOR'S **CIRCUITRY,** WHICH COULD HAVE DRAINED OFF THE POWER OF A HERALD TO **GALACTUS HIMSELF,** HAD I THE **OPPORTUNITY.**

THIS IS FOR THE **BEST,** CHILD. IT **TRULY** IS. ONLY ONE SUCH AS **MYSELF** IS **WORTHY** OF SUCH POWER.

"YES, INDEED, ALL FOR THE BEST. BEST FOR THE WORLD... FOR YOU... FOR ME...
"...FOR US. IN A WAY, YOU WILL BE LIKE A SON TO ME.
"THE SON... OF A GOD. WE WILL RULE THIS WORLD WITH NO INTERFERENCE FROM THOSE SUPER-POWERED GNATS.
"AND WE WILL DEFEAT THE CELESTIALS, FOR TRULY, AGAINST OUR COMBINED POWER, WHAT THREAT COULD THEY POSSIBLY POSE?"

GIVE ME BACK MY SON!
GET 'IM, DAD! KICK THE SNOT OUTTA 'IM!
YOU HAD EVERYTHING, VICTOR! YOU HAD FRIENDS... RESPECT...
AND YOU HAD LIFE, RICHARDS. BUT THOSE THINGS YOU ESPOUSE MEAN NOTHING TO ME...
...AND APPARENTLY, YOUR LIFE MEANS NOTHING TO YOU.
UNHAND HIM, VILLAIN. THIS BOY RETURNS TO HIS FATHER, AND THEY WILL RETURN HOME...
...EVEN IF IT COSTS ME MY IMMORTAL LIFE AND SOUL!

REED! REED, WE CAN'T LEAVE THOR BEHIND! HE'LL BE... HE'LL BE... AND DOOM --! WHAT ABOUT --?
WHAT OF ME? YOUR WOULD-BE HEROICS ACCOMPLISH NOTHING, THUNDER GOD. IF YOU AND I REMAIN BEHIND IN THIS SPHERE, ALL SHALL PERISH.
IF I MUST DIE TO TAKE ALL OF YOU WITH ME... THEN SO BE IT.
OR ELSE I SHALL SURVIVE TO RETURN TO OUR OTHER WORLD... AND RULE WITH NONE OF YOU TO STOP ME! EITHER WAY, THE FINAL TRIUMPH WILL BE MINE!
REED! SUSAN! WORRY NOT FOR THYSELVES OR FOR ME! ON MY HONOR, I SWEAR THAT NO HARM SHALL BEFALL YOU FROM DOOM'S MACHINATIONS!
WHAT ARE YOU DOING?!
USING MY HAMMER TO TAP INTO DIMENSIONAL ENERGIES... TO CREATE A RIFT IN-BETWEEN REALITIES, WHERE I SHALL HURL US BOTH...
...AND IF I AM TO SPEND ETERNITY THERE, BATTLING YOU TO MAINTAIN THE SAFETY OF TWO REALITIES... THEN THAT IS AN ETERNITY WELL SPENT! OR, TO USE THY OWN WORDS...
...SO BE IT!

WE GOT 'EM! THEY'RE BACK IN! BUT... WHERE'S THOR?!
HE... HE HAULED DOOM SOMEWHERE ELSE! I DON'T KNOW WHERE!
BUT THE CELESTIALS SAID WE HAD TO RETURN TOGETHER! DOOM AND THOR AREN'T BACK ON EARTH... BUT WE'RE SEPARATED! IS THAT ENOUGH TO --

TO BACK THEM OFF, THROW OFF THE BALANCE? I'D HAVE TO GIVE THAT A BIG "YES," REED! THE SHRINKING FIELD JUST WENT OFF-LINE!
THE SHRINKING FIELD IS SHUT DOWN! WE'RE GROWING OUT OF CONTROL! THE STRESS IS TEARING THE ENTIRE VESSEL APART!

IT'LL NEVER SURVIVE THE CROSSING! NEVER CRACK THROUGH THE --
THE BORDER! DEAD AHEAD! IT'S --

AND SUE SEES A LIFE OF WEDDED BLISS, OF HER CHILD... AND SHE IS CONTENT.

AND BRUCE SEES A LIFE OF WEDDED DISCORD, OF AN ABUSIVE FATHER, OF A YOUNG MAN ONCE CAREFREE, NOW CRIPPLED... AND HE IS STUNNED.

AND TONY SEES A LIFE OF WEAKNESS, OF JUVENILE BEHAVIOR AND DEPENDENCY... AND HE IS ANGRY.

AND STEVE SEES A LIFE OF BATTLE, OF DEDICATION, OF SERVICE TO A CAUSE... AND HE IS UNCHANGED.
THE LAST TIME THE FF APPROACHED THE BORDER THEY SAW VISIONS OF THEIR PAST LIVES. THIS TIME, ALL ABOARD EXPERIENCE THAT DISORIENTATION, THAT PLACE BETWEEN WAKEFULNESS AND DREAMS...

...AND THEN, ALL THAT THEY WERE, AND ARE, AND WILL BE...
...SHATTERS...
...AND THEY REMEMBER... EVERYTHING...

...AND THEN THEY'VE TIME FOR NOTHING ELSE... AS THE ARK SHATTERS AROUND THEIR EARS.
ENERGY CRACKLES FROM THE VERY FABRIC OF REALITY AROUND THEM, AND THEY KNOW THAT -- WITHOUT THE ARK TO WARP SPACE AROUND THEM... THEY WILL NEVER MAKE IT THROUGH.
BUT THEN THE DIMENSIONAL ENERGIES AROUND THEM SEEM TO FOCUS... TO CONCENTRATE ON ONE POINT... ONE MAN, OR ONE SET OF MEN...
...A GREEN UMBILICUS FORMS BETWEEN THEM, HAULING THEM TOWARDS ONE ANOTHER EVEN AS EACH WOULD FIGHT TO RESIST ITS PULL.

FOR MONTHS, THE HULK HAS BEEN A CHANNEL FOR THE POWER OF THE TWO UNIVERSES... A GATEWAY...
...AND NOW, THRUST INTO THE MIDST OF THE VORTEX WITH DIMENSIONAL ENERGIES CRACKLING ALL AROUND HIM, SLAMMED BACK TOGETHER AT A MOLECULAR LEVEL...
...THE FORCE OF HIS REUNION UNLEASHES THAT POWER, AND THE GATEWAY SWINGS WIDE AS A HOLE RIPS OPEN IN THE EDGE OF THE NEGATIVE ZONE.
AND WITH THE EXPLOSIVE FORCE OF AIR RUSHING TO FILL A VACUUM, THE TRAVELLERS ARE DRAWN BACK INTO THEIR HOMEWORLD, LEAPING INTO EXISTENCE ALL OVER THE WORLD...
...OR... TO PUT IT SIMPLY...

...THE HEROES... RETURN.

YOU DID NOT OBEY THE SPIRIT OF OUR AGREEMENT. WE TRUSTED YOU... AND YOU TRUSTED DOOM... AND IT WAS MISPLACED.

WHO THE DEVIL DO YOU THINK YOU ARE, Huh? YOU MADE OUR LIVES MISERABLE! YOU DISRUPTED US, TOYED WITH US!
WHO ARE YOU TO DECIDE THAT FRANKLIN HAS BEEN RUINED BY US?!

SOMEONE... WHO HAS ALSO BEEN RUINED BY YOU.
TAKE CARE... SUSAN. YOU BEAR PRECIOUS CARGO.

IN THE WORLD OF THE NEWLY RETURNED TRAVELLERS... THE RAIN HAS ALREADY CEASED. AND A BIBLICAL SIGN -- A COVENANT -- MAKES ITS CUSTOMARY APPEARANCE.

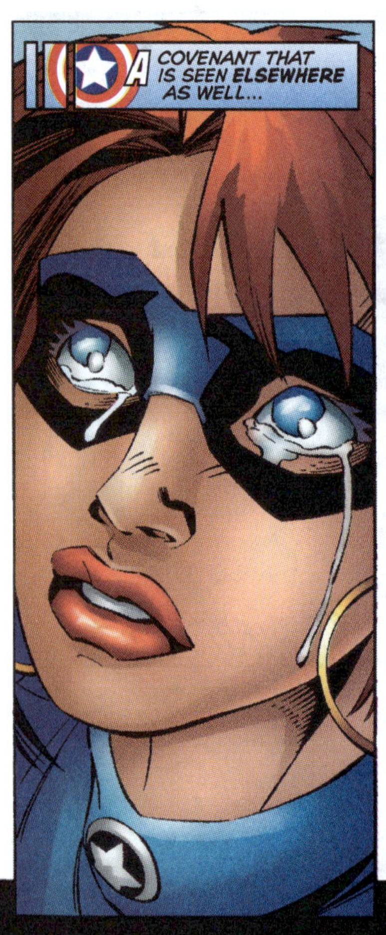
A COVENANT THAT IS SEEN ELSEWHERE AS WELL...

...AS THE ENTIRE POPULACE OF A WORLD... SAVE FOR ONE LONELY GIRL... CELEBRATES THAT THE TERROR IS OVER, THE FRIGHTENING EYES GONE, THE FIRE ABATED.

AS FOR THE GIRL...
...IT IS AS IF A DREAM WERE OVER.

THERE IS AN APPROPRIATENESS TO THAT. INDEED, IT IS BELIEVED BY SOME THAT THE WORLD... THE ENTIRE UNIVERSE...
...MERELY EXISTS AS THE DREAM OF A SLEEPING GIANT.

THAT THE GIRL -- THAT EVERYONE AND EVERYTHING --

-- IS SIMPLY THE FIGMENT OF THE IMAGINATION OF SOME GREATER BEING'S DREAM STATE.
HER NAME IS ASHEMA, AND SHE HAS BEEN PART OF AN EXPERIMENT WITH MOST STARTLING RESULTS.

AN EXPERIMENT MADE NECESSARY BY FRANKLIN'S CREATION. FRANKLIN... A BEING WHOM THE CELESTIALS FELT WAS ON PAR WITH THEMSELVES. THEY DESIRED TO TEACH HIM, TO TEST HIM.
SO ASHEMA THE LISTENER WAS CHOSEN FOR THIS ASSIGNMENT. AN ASSIGNMENT WHICH BECAME SOMETHING... UNCONTROLLED... SOMETHING SHE DID NOT EVEN FULLY COMREHEND. BUT NOW SHE DOES.
FOR IN ENTERING THE HUMAN CONDITION, SHE HAS EXPERIENCED, SHE HAS GROWN. AND AS ASHEMA HAS LEARNED, SO, TOO, DID HER FELLOW CELESTIALS.
FOR THE PURPOSE OF EXPERIMENTATION IS TO LEARN AND GROW. BUT KNOWLEDGE WITHOUT GROWTH IS A HOLLOW PURSUIT.
AND ULTIMATELY, ASHEMA SACRIFICED HER OWN CONSCIOUSNESS, GAVE IT OVER FOR THE PRESERVATION OF THE OTHER UNIVERSE, WHICH WILL EXIST WITHIN HER FOR ALL TIME.
AND THE OTHER CELESTIALS WILL STUDY HER, FEEL HER, EXPERIENCE HER... INTERNALIZED IN A WAY NEVER BEFORE POSSIBLE SINCE THEY HAD ALWAYS BEEN ON THE OUTSIDE LOOKING IN. THEIR EVOLUTION WILL TAKE EONS. BUT THE CELESTIALS HAVE NOTHING BUT TIME.

YES, THE DREAM OF A GIANT. AND PERHAPS THE CELESTIALS THEMSELVES... ARE MERELY FIGMENTS OF SOMEONE OR SOMETHING ELSE'S ETERNAL IMAGINATION.
INDEED... IN THE FINAL ANALYSIS...
...PERHAPS WE ALL ARE.
END.

HEROES REBORN: THE RETURN ISSUE 1 ALTERNATE COVER

Heroes Reborn: The Return Issue 1 Cover

HEROES REBORN: THE RETURN ISSUE 2 COVER

HEROES REBORN: THE RETURN ISSUE 2 ALTERNATE COVER

HEROES REBORN: THE RETURN ISSUE 3 COVER

HEROES REBORN: THE RETURN ISSUE 3 ALTERNATE COVER

HEROES REBORN: THE RETURN ISSUE 4 COVER

SALVADOR
S. Hanna
LIQUID!

HEROES REBORN: THE RETURN ISSUE 4 ALTERNATE COVER